IRELAND
in COLOUR

Published in Ireland by
Gill & Macmillan Ltd
Goldenbridge
Dublin 8

With associated companies around the world.

Produced in Australia by
Crawford House Publishing Pty Ltd
PO Box 1484
Bathurst NSW 2795

Featuring the photography of Hugh Watson, Bord Fáilte, and
the Northern Ireland Tourist Board.
Text and captions by David H. Barrett.

IRELAND in COLOUR

Gill & Macmillan

Ireland is a land of colour. Indeed, it can be said to have coloured the entire world. Few countries have had as wide or enduring an influence on the Western world; despite a combined population (the Republic and Northern Ireland) of just over 5 million, the culture and heritage of the tiny land has spread around the globe.

It is difficult to explain the Irish phenomenon. Perhaps it began around 300 BC when Gaelic-speaking Celts conquered Ireland, developing a culture that blossomed into artistic and literary splendour after the introduction of Christianity, traditionally in AD 432 by St Patrick. Few countries are as rich in history. Ireland is covered in castles, houses and monuments, some of which predate the Pyramids. The earliest Irish art is represented by carvings on megalithic monuments dating from between 2500 and 2000 BC.

The history and culture of the Irish are inextricable. Celtic art predominated in early historic times, from 300 BC, climaxing in illuminated manuscripts such as the *Book of Kells*. Though the basic Celtic patterns remained, works produced after the 9th century began to show European influences as Norse, Romanesque and Gothic styles were introduced by invaders such as the Vikings and Anglo-Normans. From the mid-17th century, contemporary European trends influenced the flourishing decorative arts and large-scale building.

Among the earliest surviving buildings in Ireland are the ring forts, most of which were built after the coming of Christianity in the 5th century. Hiberno-Romanesque architecture was established during the 12th century, superseded by Irish Gothic, which climaxed in the 15th century. Many 19th-century churches and buildings were influenced by this last style, during the Gothic revival. In the 20th century, cities and major towns have grown rapidly, and contemporary Irish architects strive to meet the need for modern facilities that do not compromise the integrity of the existing urban landscape.

Literature, too, is a hallmark of Irish culture. The Normans brought the English language to Ireland in the 12th century, and although Irish gradually gave way to English, it continued to exert a powerful, if subtle, influence on the English-speaking culture that was displacing it. Several highly successful literary works have been written in Irish, but literature in English by Irish authors has had the greatest impact, profoundly influencing the whole of English literature. Irish literature in English has been celebrated since the time of Jonathan Swift's *Gulliver's Travels* (1726) and Edmund Burke's *Reflections on the French Revolution* (1790). The first Irish writer to deal specifically with Irish themes was Maria Edgeworth (1767-1849). In her wake came 19th-century patriotic authors such as Thomas Davis, Samuel Ferguson and James Clarence Mangan, precursors of Irish literature's most invigorating era, the Celtic revival. This movement centred on turn-of-the-century Dublin, and included poet and playwright W.B. Yeats (who became a Nobel laureate in 1923), playwrights Lady Gregory and John Millington Synge, poets James Stephens and George Russell, and novelist George Augustus Moore.

The most celebrated Irish novelist of recent times was James Joyce (1882-1941), author of *Ulysses*. But there have been many other distinguished modern writers and poets: Flann O'Brien, Frank O'Connor, Patrick Kavanagh, Louis MacNeice, Mary Lavin, Thomas Kinsella, Nobel laureate Seamus Heaney, Elizabeth Bowen, John McGahern, and recent Booker Prize recipient Roddy Doyle.

Ireland's playwrights are also internationally renowned. During the 18th and 19th centuries, the London stage was graced by works from writers such as Oliver Goldsmith, Richard Brinsley Sheridan and the infamous Oscar Wilde. More recently, George Bernard Shaw (Nobel Prize laureate in 1935, and considered one of the greatest dramatists in the English language), Sean O'Casey, Brendan Behan, Brian Friel and Hugh Leonard have all received acclaim, as has the enigmatic Samuel Beckett, another Nobel Prize winner (1969).

But history and culture are not the only elements of colour in Ireland. Indelibly incorporated into the awe-inspiring landscape are the marks of human habitation; this blend of the natural and man-made magnificence is part of what makes Ireland so attractive.

Dublin, capital of the republic, is a low-built city whose architectural heritage is mainly Norse, Norman and Georgian. To the west lie the plains of Kildare, with evidence of early settlement, while to the south are the Wicklow Mountains, nowhere crossed at less than 300 metres (1000 feet).

The river valleys of Ireland's south-eastern corner form a rolling landscape edged by sandy beaches. Medieval Kilkenny has many magnificent buildings, including cathedrals, the town hall, and 18th-century Kilkenny Castle. Waterford is famous for its crystal factory.

The scenic south and west coasts boast the lakes of Killarney, the Ring of Kerry and Dingle Peninsula. Cork, Ireland's second city, hosts an international choral, jazz and folk-dance festival, while the nearby coast and Blarney Castle are notable attractions.

The major cities of the west coast are Limerick, straddling the River Shannon estuary, and Galway, on the northern shore of scenic Galway Bay. Connemara is typical of the west coast, with its rocky coastline, mountains, rivers, bogs and lakes. Sparsely vegetated, the Burren, in County Clare, is a distinctive region of almost horizontal limestone slabs. Scenic Donegal, with its rugged western seaboard, lies on the north-west coast. To the south is Sligo, Yeats country; many of its prominent towns and features are celebrated in his lyrics.

Northern Ireland might be thought of as a saucer, centred on Lough Neagh, whose upturned rim forms the highlands of the province. Five of its six counties meet at the lake. To the north and east are the mountains of Antrim, while the drumlins – smooth mounds created by glaciation – in the south-east culminate in the Mourne Mountains. The landscape of Northern Ireland is dotted with scattered and isolated farms, and small market towns rather than villages dominate. A few such market centres have grown into substantial towns, such as Omagh and Enniskillen in the west. Armagh, an ecclesiastical centre, is noted for its two cathedrals. Belfast, the dominant city in the region, as underlined by its size, is the centre of government, finance, education and culture in Northern Ireland.

The colours of Ireland are constantly shifting as the inexorable forces of history and culture shape and develop the land and its people. But there will always be something unique about Ireland and the Irish, something untouchable and wonderful. And that is, in essence, what Ireland is all about.

Right: The portico of the Bank of Ireland, formerly the 1729 Parliament House, Dublin.

Facing page: St Stephen's Green Centre, Dublin. St Stephen's Green, the oldest and largest of the city's squares, was recorded in 1224 as common grazing land, but is now surrounded by imposing mansions, built mainly in the 18th century.

Above: The University of Dublin (Trinity College), Ireland's oldest university, was founded in 1592 by Queen Elizabeth I, on land confiscated from a monastery, but many of its distinguished buildings were built during the 18th century. The 'Front Gate', or Regent House, was built between 1752 and 1759. Until 1792, the university remained completely Protestant, and even after Catholics were allowed entrance the Catholic Church forbade it, a restriction that remained at least partially in force until 1970. Women were first admitted in 1903, earlier than at most British universities.

Right: The 30-metre (98-foot) Campanile stands at what is thought to be the centre of the monastery that preceded Trinity College. The Campanile was designed by Edward Lanyon and built in 1852-53.

Facing page above: The neoclassical Four Courts, one of Dublin's finest monumental buildings, was designed by James Gandon and constructed between 1786 and 1802. Reduced by shellfire and mines at the outbreak of civil war in 1922, it has been rebuilt.

Facing page below: The Unitarian Church (1863) in St Stephen's Green.

Facing page above left: This Georgian doorknocker is typical of those that can be seen throughout Dublin.

Facing page above right: The pre-eminent architect of 18th-century Dublin was James Gandon. The Custom House, his first great building, was constructed between 1781 and 1791. It was gutted by fire in 1921, during the independence struggle, and the interior redesigned. This keystone on the Custom House depicts the river god.

Facing page below: Merrion Square, where these terraces are to be found, boasts an elegant central park and well-kept Georgian buildings. Dating back to 1762, it has some of the best Georgian Dublin entrances, with fine doors and peacock fanlights, and ornate doorknockers.

Left: Although seldom used today, Dublin's Grand Canal is still navigable. It enters the River Liffey at the harbour entrance, and connects with the River Shannon.

Above: The elegant Georgian doorway of the Goethe Institut Dublin, in Merrion Square.

Above: Áras an Uachtaráin ('the President's House', formerly the viceroy's lodge), Phoenix Park, Dublin.

Right: This monument to Charles Stewart Parnell stands in O'Connell Street (at first called Drogheda and then Sackville Street), Dublin. Parnell was a nationalist MP who gained great popularity in Ireland through his use of obstructive parliamentary tactics in support of Home Rule.

Facing page above: In the 12th century, the Normans built the magnificent Christ Church Cathedral on the site of an 11th-century Viking church. The cathedral fell into disrepair, and was restored at great expense in the 1870s.

Facing page below left: Fresh vegetables for sale in the markets on Moore Street, Dublin.

Facing page below right: Thomas Osborne Davis (1814-45), a writer and politician, was the chief organiser and poet of the Young Ireland movement, a nationalist group that sought to unite all creeds and classes. His writings become almost gospel to Sinn Féin. This monument stands in Dame Street, Dublin.

Left: County Wicklow includes much of the Leinster Chain mountain range, notably the Wicklow Mountains, of which one of the main valleys is that of the picturesque Glendalough (Celtic *Gleann dá Loch*, the 'glen of two lakes'). The valley is the site of one of the most significant ancient monastic settlements in the country, founded by St Kevin in the 6th century.

Above: The great Irish politician Charles Stewart Parnell was born in Avondale House (about 3 kilometres, or 2 miles, south of Rathdrum, County Wicklow) in 1846. The house dates from 1779, and contains a small museum dedicated to Parnell. The remainder of the building houses the Irish Forestry Service.

Right: The golden light of an autumn morning near Annamoe village, County Wicklow. The village is home to a trout farm, and the surrounding area is notably picturesque.

Above: The 20-hectare (49-acre) formal gardens of Powerscourt Estate, near Enniskerry, County Wicklow, have fine views of the surrounding countryside. The layout of the estate dates from the 17th and 18th centuries, while the formal gardens were laid out in the 19th century. Powerscourt House (1731) was gutted by fire in 1974, but it has been restored.

Right: Not all of Ireland's most magnificent landscapes are to be found in the west of the country. Just 16 kilometres (10 miles) south of Dublin is the wild and desolate scenery of County Wicklow.

Facing page: The Vale of Glendalough became an important monastic centre when St Kevin settled there in the 6th century. A series of churches were built in the valley during the 11th and 12th centuries. The 33-metre (108-foot) round tower was built in the 10th century.

Facing page: Tacumshin Windmill was built in 1840 by Nicholas Moran. One of Ireland's few thatched windmills, it was constructed near Tacumshin Lake, on the south-east coast of Ireland, in County Wexford.

Above: Enniscorthy, County Wexford, lies on the River Slaney, 20 kilometres (12 miles) north-west of Wexford Town. The Norman castle dates from 1205, and was a private residence until 1951.

Right: Tintern Abbey is a 12th-century Cistercian abbey in a delightful rural setting near the village of Saltmills, County Wexford. Founded by William Marshall, Earl of Pembroke, after he nearly died at sea, it is currently being restored.

Far right: This statue of a pikeman, at Vinegar Hill, commemorates the popular rising of May 1798. The rebellion met its defeat at the hill, to the east of the town of Enniscorthy.

Above: Built on the site of a medieval Norman keep on a 125-hectare (310-acre) island, Waterford Castle has the River Suir for its moat. It was held by the Fitzgerald family for many centuries, and was last extended in 1895. It was converted to a hotel in 1988.

Left: Dunmore East, County Waterford, is a busy fishing village set on a coastline of discreet coves and low, red sandstone cliffs. During summer, when there is a nightly fish market, the attractive stone harbour is packed with boats.

Above: Waterford City is most famous for the production of lead crystal, which has been manufactured there since 1783. This phase of the industry failed in 1851, when it was taxed out of existence by the British, and it was not revived until 1947. The crystal plant is 5 kilometres (3 miles) out of the city.

Above: An early-morning autumn mist lends an eerie quality to these woods in County Kilkenny.

Facing page above: A horse grazes among buttercups in the golden morning light.

Facing page below: Jerpoint Abbey, County Kilkenny, founded in 1128, is one of the finest Cistercian ruins in Ireland.

Facing page: Grogan's Bar nestles on the banks of the River Nore, Kilkenny City.
Left: Kilkenny (*Cill Chainnigh*) means 'Church of St Canice', who founded a 6th-century church on the site of St Canice's Cathedral. The cathedral was begun around 1192, and the bishop's residence was built about 1360.
Above: A brass eagle flanked by lions in St Canice's Cathedral.

Above: This farm cottage is typical of the kind seen in County Kilkenny. Rural industries are very important in the county. Principal among these are cereal-grain and vegetable growing, while dairying and beef production, and the raising of sheep, pigs and poultry, are also significant. The south-west of County Kilkenny is noted for its apples.

Right: Rothe House, a fine old Tudor house in Kilkenny City, dates from 1594. During the 1640s, Peter Rothe, the son of the original builder, had all his property confiscated for his family's part in the Confederation of Kilkenny, an anti-English Catholic alliance. His sister was later able to reclaim the house, but just before the Battle of the Boyne (1690) the family supported James II, and this time lost it permanently. It now contains a museum.

Facing page: Daly Bridge is at the western end of the island on which lies the city centre of Cork. The bridge traverses the northern channel of the River Lee, and is not far from the Cork City Gaol and Cork City Museum.

Right: St Patrick's Bridge, the termination of St Patrick's Street, Cork City, crosses the River Lee to St Patrick's Quay. The quayside, once crowded with foreign ships loading up with salted butter, now plays host to only an occasional vessel.

Overleaf: Cork City Hall, opened in 1936, replaced the previous structure, which burned down on 11 September 1920. Designed by architects Jones and Kelly, it features six limestone Tuscan pillars and a copper-domed clock tower. US president John F. Kennedy gave an address from the steps of City Hall during his triumphant 1963 tour of Ireland; the crowd in Cork was the biggest ever to gather in the city.

Facing page above: Glengarriff Harbour lies in a sheltered position at the head of Bantry Bay, County Cork. During the latter half of the 19th century, Glengarriff became a popular retreat for wealthy Victorians, who would sail from England to Ireland, then take the train to Bantry, from where a paddle steamer would take them to Glengarriff.

Facing page below: A gentle shroud of snow coats the mountains near Glengarriff.

Above: An attractive farmhouse bathed in sunshine near Glengarriff. Because of its sheltered position and the influence of the Gulf Stream, the area enjoys a particularly mild climate and a rich local flora.

Right: Crookhaven village, County Cork, is on the far side of a spur of land that runs eastward, enclosing a harbour. Crookhaven was formerly very important as a busy sailing and fishing port, and the collection point for mail from America.

Far left: Built on solid limestone, Blarney Castle, a tower house, dates from 1446. It is home to the famous Blarney Stone. The use of the word 'blarney' as an expression of dubiousness is attributed to Elizabeth I, who was exasperated by Lord Blarney's ability to talk endlessly without ever agreeing to her demands.

Left: Legend has it that those who kiss the Blarney Stone gain eloquence, or, as an 18th-century French consul put it, 'gain the privilege of telling lies for seven years'. The feat of kissing the stone can only be achieved by lying down and hanging one's head downwards, and requires a head for heights.

Below: When approaching the village of Ballydehob from the east, one can see an old, twelve-arched tramway viaduct. Ballydehob is on the Mizen Peninsula, and its name comes from the Irish *Beal Atha an dha Chab*, meaning 'the ford at the mouth of two rivers'.

Above: On the north-east of Beara Peninsula, in County Kerry, is Glanmore Lake. This area offers some magnificent scenery, including nearby 11-kilometre (7-mile) Healy Pass.

Below: The village of Allihies lies just south of copper mines opened in 1812. The mines were exporting more than 30 000 tonnes as late as the 1930s, but closed in 1962.

Above: Sunset at Ahakista, on the Sheep's Head Peninsula, County Cork. Ahakista is a tiny village with a pub, no shops, and a Japanese restaurant.

Above: The small, 15-hectare (37-acre) Garinish Island, County Cork, was made into an Italianate garden early in the 20th century. **Facing page above:** Thanks to storms, Bantry, Cork, avoided becoming the point of a French landing late in the 18th century. **Facing page below:** Healy Pass, 11 kilometres (7 miles) long, is the gateway into Kerry on the Beara Peninsula, County Cork.

Right: Ross Castle, on the shores of Lough Leane, near Killarney, County Kerry, was the last place in Munster to fall to Cromwell's forces under Ludlow. It had been prophesied that the castle would only be captured from the water. Ludlow launched floating batteries onto the lake, and the defenders, seeing the prophecy about to be fulfilled, are reported to have promptly surrendered. The castle dates back to the 14th century, when it was a residence of the O'Donoghues.

Facing page above: The Gap of Dunloe passes between Purple Mountain and Macgillycuddy's Reeks, County Kerry.
Facing page below: Idyllic scenery near the town of Sneem (pronounced 'Shneem') in the Ring of Kerry.
Above: Autumn produces a rich tapestry of gold and green along the tranquil shores of Kenmare River, County Kerry.

Facing page above: Valentia Island, 11 kilometres (7 miles) long and 3 kilometres (2 miles) wide, is a popular scuba-diving centre. It is reached by the long bridge from Portmagee, County Kerry.

Facing page below: Post office, Blackwater Bridge, County Kerry. **Above:** Castlecove village lies near the mouth of Kenmare River, County Kerry. Not far away is the 2000-year-old Staigue Fort.

Right: At either end of the Thomond Bridge, which crosses the River Shannon in Limerick City, lie significant historical sites. On the east bank of the river is St John's Castle, built at the beginning of the 13th century on the site of an earlier fortification. The castle became the most formidable bastion of English power in the west of Ireland. On the opposite bank of the river is the Treaty Stone, which marks the spot on where the Treaty of Limerick was signed in 1691, ending Limerick's resistance to the forces of William III. That the English subsequently reneged on the treaty, which guaranteed religious freedom for Irish Catholics, still rankles in Limerick.

Above: Adare Manor, County Limerick, was built by the Earl of Dunraven in 1832, and is now a hotel.

Facing page above: Knappogue Castle (1467), just south of Quin, County Clare, was used as a base by Cromwell in 1649.

Facing page below: North of Newmarket-on-Fergus, County Clare, on 220 hectares (544 acres) of gardens, is Dromoland Castle.

Above: Killaloe, County Clare, is one of the main crossings on the River Shannon. From there, the Shannon is navigable all the way up to Lough Key, County Sligo.
Right: In northern Clare, between Kinvara and Corofin, is the extraordinary and unique Burren region, a craggy limestone landscape known as karst, after a similar region in Slovenia. The name is derived from the Irish *Boireann*, 'rocky place'. One of Cromwell's generals said of the Burren that there is 'neither water enough to drown a man, nor a tree to hang him, nor soil enough to bury him' – testament not only to the appearance of the region, but also to his attitude towards the Irish.

Facing page: Kylemore Abbey, nestled in the shadow of Dúchruach Mountain, was built by 19th-century English businessman Mitchell Henry. During World War I, a group of Benedictine nuns fled Ypres, Belgium, eventually settling in Kylemore and converting it to an abbey. The nuns still run an exclusive convent school there.

Above: Clifden, capital of Connemara, is at the head of Clifden Bay, about 80 kilometres (50 miles) west of Galway City. The town sits astride the Owenglen River, in the shadow of the sharp-peaked quartzite range, the Twelve Bens, to the east.

Right: North-west of Galway City is the wild and barren Connemara region. Ice-scoured and rock-strewn, it is mostly covered with peat bog. It is known for its austerely magnificent scenery, a patchwork of bogs, pale grey mountains, lonely valleys, and small brown lakes.

Facing page above: This modest cottage of stone and thatch recalls a bygone era in Connemara.

Facing page below: While this pub in Connemara is obviously built in a much more modern style than the cottage above, it is another fine example of the thatcher's craft.

Above: The huge and imposing Catholic Cathedral of Our Lady Assumed into Heaven and St Nicholas, known for short as St Nicholas' Cathedral, or Galway Cathedral, was opened in 1965.

Right: The western part of County Galway is renowned as a wild, rugged area of immense natural beauty.

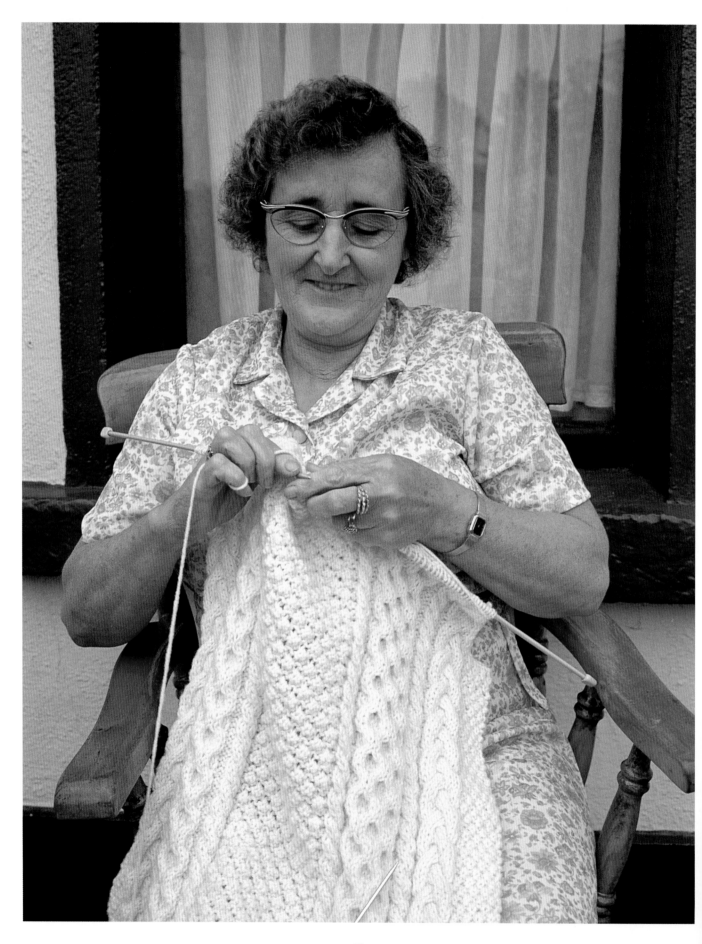

Facing page: The isolation of the Aran Islands (*Oileáin Árainn*), County Galway, allowed traditional Irish culture to survive there when it had all but died out elsewhere. Irish is still the native tongue, and traditional Aran dress was worn there until recently. The Aran sweater, knitted in white wool with marvellously complex patterns, was created on the islands.

Above: Tucked away on the south-east corner of Galway Bay is the village of Kinvara, with its small stone harbour. A quaint and relatively quiet village, it is only a few kilometres east of the Burren region in County Clare.

Right: The three Aran Islands – Inishmór, Inishmaan and Inisheer – are part of the same stretch of limestone that created the Burren region. The smallest of the islands is timeless Inisheer, the south of which is a maze of fields and sandy lanes without a building in sight.

Above: Westport House, in Westport, County Mayo, was built in 1730 on the site of an O'Malley castle on the Carrowbeg River. **Facing page above:** Ballina, County Mayo, famous for its fishing, is on the River Moy, one of the richest salmon rivers in Europe. **Facing page below:** Killala, County Mayo, reputedly founded by St Patrick, was the site of an ill-fated French invasion in 1798.

Facing page: Cheerful 17th-century thatched farmhouses in County Mayo. The county is part of the province of Connaught, in western and north-western Ireland, one of the most isolated and ruggedly beautiful parts of the country.

Right: Monasterboice, County Louth, about 10 kilometres (6 miles) north of Drogheda, is an intriguing monastic site said to have been founded by St Buithe in the 4th or 5th century. It contains a cemetery, two ancient church ruins, one of the tallest and best round towers in Ireland, and two of the finest high crosses. Muiredach's Cross, illustrated, dates from early in the 10th century. The carvings on the face shown here relate mainly to the New Testament, depicting, from the bottom, the arrest of Christ, Doubting Thomas, Christ handing a key to St Peter, the Crucifixion in the centre, and Moses praying with Aaron and Hur. A gable-roofed church caps the cross. The other face relates mainly to the Old Testament.

Above: Ben Bulben (527 metres, or 1730 feet) is part of the spectacularly scarped Dartry Mountains, County Sligo.
Below: The rocky shores of Drumcliff Bay, County Sligo.

Facing page above: Markree Castle (17th century), near Collooney, County Sligo, is now a hotel.
Facing page below: Puckaun village, north-west County Tipperary.

Above: Stone bridge at Creeslough, a small village near an inlet of Sheep Haven Bay, in the north-west of County Donegal.
Facing page above: Fishing fleet off Burtonport, County Donegal, home to the 1970s commune known as 'the Screamers'.
Facing page below: The long, sandy beach at Portnoo, on the southern side of Gweebarra Bay, County Donegal.

Right: Mount Errigal, 752 metres (2467 feet), is the highest peak of the Derryveagh range, one of the two main ranges in County Donegal.

Above: Stone warehouses at Ramelton (founded early in the 17th century), on the Rosguill Peninsula, County Donegal.
Facing page above: The Pier Bar at Portsalon, County Donegal.

Portsalon boasts a stretch of golden sand that is safe for swimming.
Facing page below: Glengesh Pass, a stunningly beautiful glacial valley between Glencolumbcille and Ardara, County Donegal.

Facing page above: Stormont, in Belfast, built in neoclassical style in 1932, was home to the Northern Ireland Parliament until 1972.
Facing page below: The Queen's College building of Queen's University, Belfast, was completed in 1849.
Above: The view from the top of St Patrick's Roman Catholic Cathedral (1838-73) in Armagh, ecclesiastic capital of Ireland.

Facing page: Straddling the border of counties Tyrone and Derry are the gentle contours of the Sperrin Mountains, 64 kilometres (40 miles) from east to west. The open moorland of the upper reaches, with its blanket bog and heather, contrasts with the wooded valleys and farmland of the lower slopes.

Above: One of the gates of the walled city of Derry. The walls were built between 1613 and 1618, which makes it the last walled city built in Ireland. The walls are about 8 metres (26 feet) high, 9 metres (29 feet) thick, and 1.5 kilometres (nearly a mile) long. The four original gates have been restored, and three new gates added.

Left: Ulster History Park, 10 kilometres (6 miles) north-east of Omagh, County Tyrone, portrays the history of Ireland from the Stone Age to the plantation (the colonisation policy pursued by Elizabeth I and James I of England). The park features full-scale models of a Mesolithic encampment, Neolithic houses, a late Bronze Age crannóg (artificial island built for defence), a 12th-century church settlement complete with round tower, and a Norman motte-and-bailey.

Above: The Mourne Mountains, County Down, have long held out against human settlement. Even today, surrounded on all sides by villages and towns, they are crossed by only one road. The steep, craggy peaks have not been as affected by glaciation as other similar ranges, so there are no low, polished hills here. The mountains are perhaps best-known through the words of Percy French, according to whom they 'sweep down to the sea'.

Right: Built in the 1760s by Lord and Lady Bangor, Castleward House is a unique mixture of neoclassical and Gothic styles. The strange combination came about because Bernard Ward (Lord Bangor) and his wife, Anne, had completely different tastes. Bernard favoured the neoclassical Palladian approach (seen on the front facade and classical staircase), while Anne leant towards Strawberry Hill Gothic (the back facade and her fan-vaulted boudoir).

Facing page above: Sea fishing in Northern Ireland is mainly confined to the northern Irish Sea along the coast of County Down. The primary fishing ports are Kilkeel, Ardglass and Portavogie, and prawns, cod, whiting and herring are among the main catches.

Facing page below: Although the high season for tourism in Ireland is July and August, there is much to be said for winter, during which one can view such idyllic scenes as this rustic cottage surrounded by a soft blanket of snow in County Derry.

Above: The Giant's Causeway, in County Antrim, is a geographical formation comprising some 37 000 hexagonal basalt columns (including the ones underwater). Legend has it that the giant Finn McCool wanted stepping stones to the Scottish island of Staffa, where similar rock formations can be seen. The scientific explanation is that around 60 million years ago, red-hot lava erupted from a subterranean fissure and crystallised into the unusual shapes. The mountain in the background is Aird Snout.

Right: Picturesque Ballintoy, County Antrim, is a small harbourside village a few kilometres east of the Giant's Causeway.